AND GOD BLESS UNCLE HARRY AND HIS ROOMMATE JACK,

WHO WE'RE NOT SUPPOSED TO TALK ABOUT

Cartoons from <u>Christopher Street</u>

AND GOD BLESS UNCLE HARRY AND HIS ROOMMATE JACK,

WHO WE'RE NOT SUPPOSED TO TALK ABOUT

Cartoons from Christopher Street

AVON
PUBLISHERS OF BARD, CAMELOT AND DISCUS BOOKS

AND GOD BLESS UNCLE HARRY AND HIS ROOMMATE JACK, WHO WE'RE NOT SUPPOSED TO TALK ABOUT is an original publication of Avon Books. This work has never before appeared in book form.

AVON BOOKS
A division of
The Hearst Corporation
959 Eighth Avenue
New York, New York 10019

Copyright © 1978 by That New Magazine, Inc.
Published by arrangement with That New Magazine, Inc.
Library of Congress Catalog Card Number: 77-99102
ISBN: 0-380-01897-7

All rights reserved, which includes the right
to reproduce this book or portions thereof in
any form whatsoever. For information address
Jane Rotrosen, 212 East 48 Street
New York, New York 10017

First Avon Printing, April, 1978

AVON TRADEMARK REG. U.S. PAT. OFF. AND IN
OTHER COUNTRIES, MARCA REGISTRADA, HECHO EN
U.S.A.

Printed in the U.S.A.

"And God bless Uncle Harry and his roommate Jack, who we're not supposed to talk about."

"If you ask me, I think we had more fun when it was unnatural."

"I drag you out of the sea. I build a shelter for you. I hunt for food. And now you tell me you're a lesbian."

"Now that's Camp!"

"After a hard day at the office, it's nice to be with your own kind, isn't it?"

"Must you always look as though you're available at fine stores everywhere?"

"I love waking up in the morning and finding you there beside me."

"I must confess, you did look better in the bar."

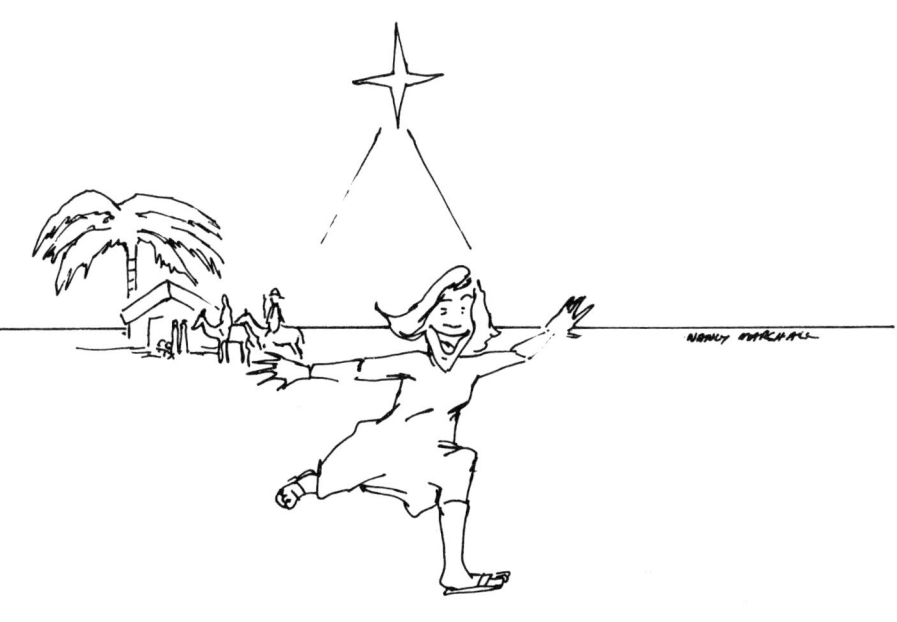

"It's a girl!"

"Henry, you know that phase little Hank was going through? Well, it just turned into a *lifestyle*."

"We must be getting close to the Village."

"That's okay, Ms. Williams, come in. There's nothing more satisfying than putting an ex-lover on hold."

"Why can't we write in a gay character?"

"Honestly, Mitchell, I can tell the difference between loving you and loving your apartment."

"Look, I'm just as nervous about this as you are."

"I know we're supposed to be more sentitive, but this is ridiculous."

"Actually, there are only twenty lesbians in New York. It's all done with mirrors."

"Morris, you can take credit for his homosexuality, but I've got dibs on his chutzpah."

"Okay, so you bought the violets after Alice left you for Kate, and you bought the asparagus ferns after you broke up with Ginnie, and you got the hydrangea after Linda went into the convent, and you purchased the coleus when Fran left you for that young graduate from Sarah Lawrence, but that still leaves the philodendrons: I want the dirt on the philodendrons."

"Her closet's got a revolving door."

"Don't bother coming down tonight. The place is full of trolls."

"Since I don't intend to come out until I'm very rich and very old, let's sing some of those fabulous heterosexual songs of yesteryear."

"Oh yeah, Arthur and I do have simultaneous orgasms—but in different cities."

"... And now I'd like to introduce the woman who organized the lesbian world into two softball teams..."

"I hope this relationship doesn't last too long. I left the motor running."

"I understand they're under new management."

"I'm in the mood for like."

"Your milieu or mine?"

ALICE "HOT SHOT" BARNES, WHO PRIDES HERSELF IN POCKETING SEVERAL BALLS WITH ONE PERFECT SHOT, FINDS THAT HER NEWLY-ACQUIRED LOVER, SONJA, IS AN ENTHUSIASTIC, BUT TOTALLY INEPT POOL-PLAYER, IN FULL VIEW OF TWO OF ALICE'S EX-LOVERS.

"Aren't you taking our Platonic relationship a little too far?"

"Gee, you're right, this is the only place we've never done it!"

"If you're Judy, you're an hour early. If you're Alice, you're a day late. If you're Betty, you can pick up your toothbrush and beat it."

"It's better than waiting three hours in a smoke-filled bar for it."

"Roger, tell me 99 things you like about me."

"Dear Miss Barker,
Congratulations! This is to inform you that, with the recent death of
Miss Gracie Ellsworth of Cape Girardeau, Mo.,
you are now the oldest living lesbian in the United States..."

"I know that art department is gay, but is it gay enough?"

"Who would ever have thought that the treasure at the end of your rainbow would turn out to be me?"

"We're calling it 'Oklahomosexual.'"

"Oh, it wasn't as early as 'Sgt. Pepper'—I didn't come out until 'Abbey Road'!"

"If Henry Bassett from West Tenth Street is in there, somebody please tell him that he is part of a relationship that no longer exists."

"When you walked in here, there was something about you that said 'East 57th Street.'"

"Too bad you left me twenty years ago, Monica. We could have been great together."

"Yes, I'm alone—in the Biblical sense of the word."

"One can't be too careful these days."

"Peter may be gay, but he's still a family man."

"I bought them to keep my mind off the bars."

"Hi. It's just us, the neighboring homosexuals."

"I worship the ground you hype on."

"We're here today to talk to a blue-collar worker about homosexuality among the working classes."

"Mom and Dad, this is my new lover. He'r rather remain anonymous, but for the purpose of identification, let's call him Tom."

"Hello, Benny. It's your mother. I only have a minute. Get married, have children. Goodbye."

"Sorry, I'm only available on a stand-by basis."

"But to fall in love with you would be taking the easy way out."

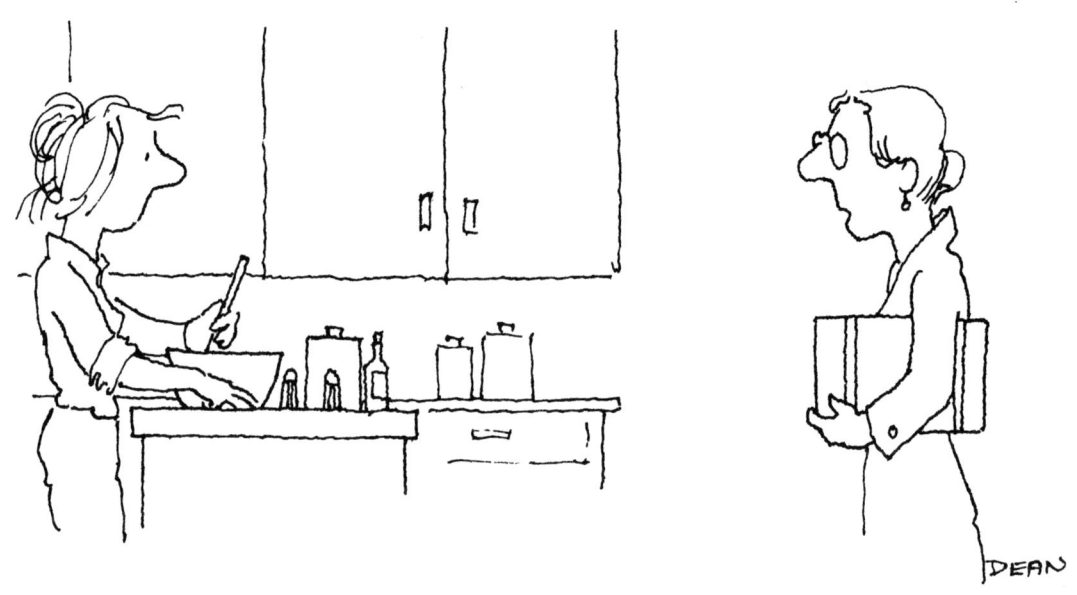

"I know you've probably heard this one before, but how would you like to go to Puerto Rico for the weekend?"

"At least you're not walking out on me!"

"And what if Jill Johnston doesn't like younger women?"